I0004764

Legal Disclaimer

The author of this book is not an attorney and makes no claim to be one. The information in this book does not create or constitute a client relationship. The materials presented in this book are based solely on the experiences of the author.

Table of Contents

FORWARD

I want to thank you very much for purchasing **MS Word Legal – *Awareness Explosion* Volume 2 along with your bonus material in the back!** This book represents an additional portion of the 6 years of articles that I have contributed to various blogs. This series of books will give you **an accurate window** into what it is like to work in a top-tier legal word processing training center. Volumes 1 and 2 go over a tremendous amount of material. Each successive article is very different from the one before and each book covers a ton of ground. They are fun to read and the material is easy to understand and absorb. *This is information that you can use right away rather than someday.* You can think of this book as going to "**Legal Word Processing School**" where you just have to read the easy flowing articles. It really makes no difference whether you have MS Word open in front of you or not. Either way, through our narrative style, you will be exposed to numerous scenarios, explanations, and solutions that will help you to grow as an operator or secretary.

Your awareness level will continue to sky rocket! You can read technical books **ALL DAY** but you will not be exposed to the diverse amount of material that will comfortably unfold before you in this book.

This book can be used as a study guide for people trying to get into the legal business, people already in the legal business who want to expand their awareness, students as well as those new to working within a legal environment. This is also a great series for job agency counselors and those working for single practitioners and smaller offices, to provide a good and accurate feel of the day to day interactions and subject matter encountered within a large law firm.

I found that blogs move very fast in that an article that I write today will be way down the line and out of sight within a few days and in some cases a few hours. Nevertheless, the information that I touch upon is vital and important and through the medium of self publishing, I can reach and help an exponential amount of people.

I write the articles I do because I see too much generic talk and wanted to make sure that people deal with and see what really goes on from day to day the good and sometimes stressful. Think of this series as a great expansion of your knowledge base. Feel free to follow me on **legaltestready.com** and on Twitter **@legaltestready**. Through that site you can contact us for basic-advanced Legal MS Word Training. We do public training, test creation as well as transforming legal firms large and small with our style of training.

Best regards,

Louis

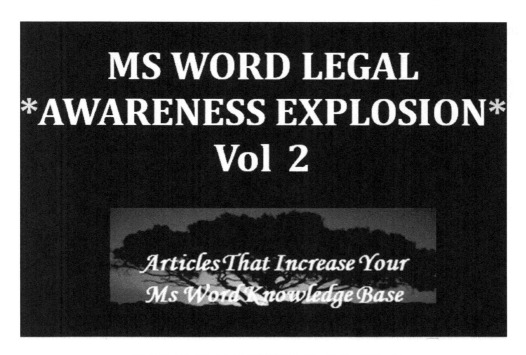

MS WORD LEGAL *AWARENESS EXPLOSION* Vol 2

Articles That Increase Your Ms Word Knowledge Base

ARTICLES FROM YESTERDAY AND TODAY

I.   Articles Relating to Working In A Legal Word Processing Center

Object Linking And Embedding

This is a very good link to help familiarize you in terms of Object Linking and Embedding such as an object or picture directly linked to an Excel File. If you have not done this before, you will understand why it is utilized.

http://office.microsoft.com/en-us/excel-help/create-edit-and-control-ole-objects-HP010217697.aspx
Create, edit, and control OLE objects office.microsoft.com

........*

Make Good Use Of Your Status Bar

In MS Word 2003, we took for granted that the Status Bar on the bottom of your screen would always display certain info such as **Formatted Page Number, Section, Page Number, Vertical Page Position, Line Number etc.**

Depending on the workstation you sit down at will determine what items in the Status bar are active. It is simple enough to turn on whatever you need by right clicking on the Status Bar (at the very bottom of your screen) and check off what you want.

Customize Status Bar		
√	Formatted Page Number	2
√	Section	4
√	Page Number	6 of 38
	Vertical Page Position	3.1"
	Line Number	8
√	Column	1
√	Word Count	13,710
	Number of Authors Editing	
√	Spelling and Grammar Check	Checking
√	Language	
√	Signatures	Off
√	Information Management Policy	Off
√	Permissions	Off
	Track Changes	Off
√	Caps Lock	Off
√	Overtype	Insert
√	Selection Mode	
√	Macro Recording	Not Recording

1.   I think that **Section, Formatted Page Number** and **Page Number** are essential. Knowing what Section your cursor is currently in is important info, while knowing what page you are on within the document as a whole vs. what a particular page is set up to display in terms of page number is also important info.

2.   For those who worked with 2003 you always had **REC, TRK, OVR** and **EXT** waiting for you on your status bar. Double Clicking on **REC** would allow you to start recording a macro, **TRK** would turn on Track Changes, **OVR** would activate **Overstrike** and **EXT** would turn on your **Extended Highlighting Feature.**

3.   If you look on the current Status Bar they are all still available and "**Selection Mode**" is the new term for Extended Highlighting.

4.   For those of you who are curious about **Extended Highlighting** you usually need a standard keyboard to use it. I have not had that much luck using a laptop keyboard. Well, here it goes. On 2003, if you turned on the EXT button or F8 Key on the status bar then anything you touched on the keyboard it would highlight up to the first instance of whatever you selected. So, if I activated Extended Highlighting and pressed the Return Key 3x the system would highlight the first 3 paragraphs. Remember any thing you touch it highlights up to the first instance of whatever key you touch. Turn on Extended Highlighting and press the period key to highlight a sentence at a time . Turn on Extended Highlighting and do Control Shift End to highlight from the cursor position to the end of the doc. Remember it works from the position of the cursor forward.

5.   So, to use Extended Highlighting in post 2003 press your **F8 key** and that will activate it. F8 or Esc. key to turn it off. It is very useful for pinpoint highlighting. Remember on many laptops the F8 will not turn on the Extended Highlighting but the standard keyboard should work.

........*

Rotating Text In MS Word and Wrapping Text In PowerPoint

Until MS Word 2010 we were able to do the following:

1.   If we needed to rotate text we could use the **Text Art** feature. After typing the text you would then have the ability to rotate the text as needed. You could not use this for everything since "**Text Art**" has a distinct look and good for specific things relating to graphics such as **Logos, Headings, Mastheads**, etc.

2.   If you are doing a table with many columns we sometimes rotate text in the table headings (each separate cell), to display the headings vertically in order to save room or as a specific look. For this, we make use of the "**Text Direction**" **button** under the **Layout Tab** under "**Table Tools**" when using tables. The **Text Direction Button** looks like this:

3.   Up until 2013, if you placed text in a text box or object, and used the rotate feature the text box or object would rotate but the text would stay still and **NOT** rotate.

4.   Finally, in 2013, MS Word, you can now place your text in a text box or object and the text will rotate along with the text box or object. This makes things a lot easier and it works great!

........*

Wrapping Text Around A Picture or Object in PowerPoint:

The situation: You bring a picture or an object into a PowerPoint slide. You need the text that is in the slide to wrap around the picture. Well, what a pain in 2003-10. In order to do so, you have to send the picture or object to the back then bring in multiple text boxes and manually manipulate the text by hand using the spacebar in order to achieve the look of text wrapping around the object.

You would be better off just doing it in word and snap shoting the text and picture then bringing the snapshot into PowerPoint.

Someone at Microsoft obviously picked up on this problem. **Auto-Text Wrapping in Power Point now exits!**

When an image is added to a slide with text in it, the text automatically readjusts itself around the image so that there is no overlapping of any kind."

Check this out and try this out. Once you see what you had to do from PowerPoint 2003-10 you will really appreciate this feature.

........*

Signature Blocks When Pressed For Time

I have discussed signature blocks before, where I have recommended having signature blocks sitting in a template in various scenarios if the firm does not have a macro or template.

I have recommended having the traditional signature set up and ready to go. By traditional, I mean the Signature style that automatically throws the signature to **3.0** on the ruler as well as having signature blocks waiting in tables for those scenarios where you have two columns of signatures.

What if you are really under pressure and you do not have signatures ready to go but nevertheless you have a number of signatures to get in place?

1.   It does not matter whether you use signatures within tables or outside of tables -- what I am going to show you will speed up the process. Most of you will say "of course" but I have seen (because of pressure) or someone like an attorney hanging over your shoulder a minor but critical mistake that people make that really slows one down and only adds to an already stressful situation.

2.   Let's assume you are doing signatures in tables. Two columns Making use of Soft Returns (shift enter) and Hard Returns.

¤	By:_____·Soft·return↵	¤
	Name:·soft·return↵	
	Title:·Hard·Return¶	
	¤	
¤	¤	¤

3.   As soon as you have one good signature, in the format that you see below, you then copy the good one to all the other slots in the table that need a signature.

By:_____Soft·return↵	By:_____Soft·return↵	¤
Name:·soft·return↵	Name:·soft·return↵	
Title:·Hard·Return¶	Title:·Hard·Return¶	
¤	¤	
By:_____Soft·return↵	By:_____Soft·return↵	¤
Name:·soft·return↵	Name:·soft·return↵	
Title:·Hard·Return¶	Title:·Hard·Return¶	
¤	¤	

4.   The problem occurs with **tables** when instead of a **Hard Return** at the end of the word Title, you have a "**Table**" return instead. In this scenario each time you try to copy a completed signature to another cell **your signature will collapse**.

5.   In order to copy a completed signature from one cell to another smoothly (meaning it stays intact), remember that *only the hard return holds instruction regarding formatting and* table cell symbols *do not*. So, when highlighting the signature to be copied, just remember to always "include" the hard return after Title when copying a signature and you will be done quickly.

Try it out and you will see how easy it is for you to produce signature blocks.

........*

Know What Controls The TOC, TOA and Index of Terms

Part of my training involves running a **TOC, TOA and Index of Terms**. What I attempt to do is to get the student to look at each newly run TOC, TOA and Index of Terms as something that can and should be modified as needed through the styles associated with each.

What I do see people do is to manually manipulate (direct formatting) the TOC for example in order to adjust spacing between each heading, correct the spacing between the heading text and the page number and on and on. Although it may do the trick for the moment and the attorney is happy, the moment that the TOC in this case is re-run (**updated**) the problems that you dealt with using direct formatting will now **resurface** and you are back to the same situation. So let's go over what controls what?

TOC - The styles associated with the completed TOC are **TOC 1, TOC 2 etc**. If you are in **Draft View**, you may wish to double click on TOC1 sitting in the style area (left side) for instance to gain access to modify. You can also do **Control + Shift + S** in order to search out the needed style and then modify as needed.

TOA - well, the actual completed TOA entries are controlled by the style "**Table of Authorities**". The **headings** of the TOA (**Cases, Statutes, Rules**) are controlled by the style "**TOA Heading**". Note: Most often you need to modify TOA Heading because the font of the TOA Heading is not generically in Times New Roman. If you check it out, you will certainly see what I mean.

Index of Terms- The completed index entries are controlled by the style "**Index**.

All the styles will always be staring at you on the left side of your screen if you are in "Draft view", and your **Style area width is set to 1 inch under Format - Options - Advanced–Display**.

Point being, is if you need to modify the completed TOC, TOA or Index of Terms **doing it through styles takes care of it for good**. In this way, it **does not** put another secretary or operator back in the same position you were in before you did your edits of the TOC, TOA and Index. Always plan ahead for others who might work on the same document after you are gone for the day.

........*

Adding A Font To A Particular Computer

Recently, I had a situation where we had a Fancy Font that we really liked on a Lenovo laptop. Pulling the same document up on the Asus laptop, the Logo being developed did not look the same -- not even close. For whatever reason, both laptops did not share the "same" standard fonts. So, we copied the Font we needed from the Lenovo machine and threw it on a thumb drive whereby we then uploaded it on the other laptop. This happens more than you might think.

1.   For example: Someone uses an offbeat font for a Power Point presentation. They send it to the client or travel to an event where when displayed, does not look as intended due to the workstation or laptop not sharing the same font. In those cases you either have to include the font in the email for the client to upload and in the case of an event have the font on a thumb drive so you can upload it as needed.

2.   If you go on Google, there are many sites that offer custom fonts and different fonts other than the usual. Personally the standard list is quite thorough.

So let's go through the uploading of a font to whatever operating system you may have.

To install a font on Windows 8

1.	Open Fonts by clicking the Start button.

2.	Click Control Panel.

3.	Click Appearance and Personalization

4.	Click Fonts.

5.	Click File, and then click Install New Font.

6.	In the Add Fonts dialog box, under Drives, click the drive where the font that you want to install is located and select it to complete the process.

I Get It Now, Old Vs. New Style Separator

A while back I posted a thorough article about the style separator. Let me refresh your memory about the style separator that was introduced in MS Word 2003.

You have a Multi-Level outline going. Let's say level one (Heading 1) is Article 1. and level 2 (Heading 2) of the outline is Section 1.1

Now, in many documents that use outlining, the headings are by themselves and do not share the regular paragraph. Sometimes they do, and when they do, the majority of the time it is the second level. It would look something like this:

Section 1.1 Provisions of the Contract. Paragraph text... Paragraph text... Paragraph text... Paragraph text... Paragraph text... Paragraph text... Paragraph text... Paragraph text... Paragraph text... Paragraph text... Paragraph text...

Because Section 2 **shares** the paragraph, if we **do not** put in the Style Separator between the end of the Heading 2 paragraph and the body text of that paragraph, (**control alt enter**) when we run the TOC, it will bring in the entire paragraph into the TOC.

Without going through the entire Style Separator routine, how did they go about this **before the current style separator** when they were in a position of Heading 2 sharing the paragraph?

1.	They would apply heading two which would temporarily apply to the entire paragraph.

2.	Then they made a return after the second level info which would throw the bulk of the paragraph underneath the level two heading.

3.   They would then highlight the return (just the return) they just made and apply the "hidden" attribute to it (under Font) and would color the return red so other operators are tipped off that this method is in use.

4.   They would then highlight the remainder of the paragraph and apply a body text that served to disassociate the remainder of the paragraph from the Heading 2 even though heading two shares the paragraph. When the TOC is run the Heading 2 text will only be extracted.

5.   This method does work but it is essentially not used because of the way it displays visually on the screen.

Okay so what do we want to take from this?

1.   With the current style separator, the paragraph stays together and appears as one solid paragraph at all times both on the screen and in the Print Preview and Print Layout.

1.1 → Formation. A limited·liability·company·(the·"Company")·has·been·formed· pursuant· to· the· Ohio· Limited· Liability· Company· Act· (_____·, Ohio· Revised·Statutes)·(the·"Act").·The·terms·and·provisions·of·this·Agreement·shall·be·construed·and· interpreted·in·accordance·with·the·terms·and·conditions·of·the·Act.¶

2.   With the old method, the bulk of each second level paragraph appears under the Heading Level 2 text on the screen.

1.1 → Formation.¶

·A·limited·liability· company·(the·"Company")·has·been· formed·pursuant·to·the·Ohio·Limited· Liability·Company·Act·(_____·,Ohio·Revised·Statutes)·(the·"Act").·The· terms· and·provisions· of·this·Agreement·shall· be·construed·and·interpreted·in·accordance·with·the· terms·and·conditions·of·the·Act.¶

3.   With the old method, because the return uses the "**Hidden**" attribute, when you go to Print Layout or look at the paragraph under Print Preview, "**only then**" will the paragraph look as one solid paragraph.

4.   On the regular screen, it will always look like it has been separated from the Heading 2 line and this confusing look I believe is what prompted Microsoft to create the Style Separator.

........*

8

When It's Already Part of The Numbering System

Cross References:

To start off, the basic essence of the cross reference is the following:

The Cross Reference feature is constantly asking what number is presently next to the paragraph that I am referencing and making sure that the outline number sitting next to the paragraph I am referencing within the document "right now", matches the number of the paragraph you are referring to in the corresponding cross reference. Same idea for page number Cross References.

As you know, when using Multi Level Outline Numbers, if you placed the word "**Article**" or "**Section**" before the **auto number field code,** then the words Article or Section are now considered part of the number for that level. So look at the sample below which shows a full context Cross Reference:

"Issuance Date" means any Trading Day during the Commitment Period that an Issuance Notice is deemed delivered pursuant to Section 2.03(b) hereof.

Above is the sample cross reference.

1.   In the case above, if the word "Section" of **Section 2.03** is actually part of the 2nd level number of the Multi-Level Outline, you **do not need to type the word "Section"** within the text of your paragraph because when the Cross Reference comes in, it will be part of the **Section 2.03(b)** cross reference.

2.   If in the same sample paragraph above, the word "**Section**" is **NOT** part of the numbering system in your Multi-Level Outline Dialog box, then you "hard type" the word "Section" then go to cross references and insert Reference to "**Paragraph Number (full context)**", the reference type is "**Numbered Item**" and the grey area will now come in as **2.03(b)**

3.   Remember, you will see your grey fields provided you have your Field Shading on under **File-Option-Advanced-Show Document Content**. I personally use the "**always**" selection.

4.   It is good to operate with the "**Field Shading On**" option because you will then see all your automated items such as your page numbering, outline level numbering, list numbering, generated TOC, TOA, Index of Terms and of course Cross References.

Cross References can be very easy to use once you are comfortable with the concept.

........*

Setting The Page Numbering

THE PAGE NUMBERING FOR THE 2007-13 USERS

For the 2007-13 users: In order to **hold off the page number** on the first page of the actual document (the main part of the document) and **start the numbering on the second page footer** of the actual document as **2** do the following:

Under the "**Insert Tab**" choose Footer. Under the 3 template footer scenarios choose Edit Footer

Make sure you turn off **Link To Previous** right away.

Make sure **Different First Page** is checked on.

Look for the **Page Number button** (left side).

Go in there and look for "**Format Page Number**".

Make it **1,,2,3** style of numbering and choose **Start at 1**.

Select OK.

Immediately navigate to the footer that sits at the bottom of page 2 of the main part of the document.

Select **Page Number** again and "Current Position", choose **the plain text option** which is the top scenario. This initially brings in the number on the left side (if you had not already centered the cursor) and then when the number comes in, simply click on your center icon and that will place the number in the center of the footer. Your numbering will come in as 2 and your page numbering will now be set for the remainder of the section. You can also, 1) center your cursor first, then 2) go into your Page Number button, 3) go to Current Position and 4) choose the plain text option.

........*

Removing The Ability To Expand

As part of my teaching, we always go over the Caption Box and other instances where for a particular style or look, they make use of the colon (:) or the parenthesis usually the closed parenthesis for stylistic purposes.

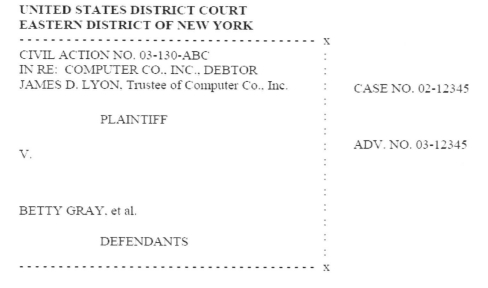

Another example would be:

Situations where between signature blocks, you may have a narrow column filled with parenthesis that serve as a stylistic type separator between the two signature blocks.

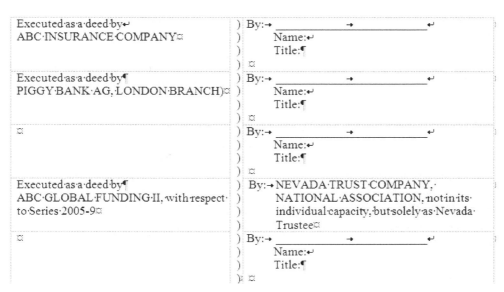

The point is that when you take an agency test or you do this at work you should remove the selection "Automatically Resize To Fit Contents" which is found under Table Properties (Options)

1.   The column that is designated for the Colons or the closed parenthesis is intentionally squeezed down to accommodate one character.

2.   When you start putting in the colons etc., if you do not turn off the above mentioned selection, then you need to place a soft or hard return after each and every instance since the cell will want to expand to accommodate each new character.

3.   As soon as you remove the selection "Automatically Resize To Fit Contents" then you can simply type one colon or parentheses after another and each one will automatically fall under the previous one since the cell can no longer expand. Soft or hard returns are no longer necessary once you do this.

4.   Finally, to disable "Automatically Resize To Fit Contents" select your entire table, right click and go to **Table Properties**. Go to **Options** and unclick the selection. Knowing this piece of info can gain a few points on a test and an edge at work if you need to show this to a co-worker.

........*

Simple But Effective

This article has to do with Labels that were generated as a result of a Merge.

Many firms use an MS Word Table or Excel Table to store the Names and Addresses that will be used for each individual Merge letter or each individual label that is generated to go along with each letter.

The first item has to do with the spacing between each line of the address once the label sheets are generated. Many times the labels are generated with a line of space between each line of the address.

1.   You can select the table (use target symbol that pops up on the left side of table in print layout view) and remove the "before and after" spacing (under Paragraph) which will tighten up the addresses. You will have to do this each time you rerun the merge. Sometimes it will not matter if there is a space between each line of text. But, it will matter when there is a lot of detail to each address and sometimes dropping the font to a smaller size is also necessary just to get all the info on the label. **2x4 labels are very popular** in law firm settings.

2.   To help remedy the spacing between the lines issue, in your MS Word data table, you can use soft returns (shift + enter) after each line of each address with the exception of the last line.

3.   When you generate the merge, you will No Longer have the extra space between each line of your address.

4.   For your Excel data document, the equivalent to the soft return is "**Alt Enter**" but when generated it still seems to come in with extra space. If so, just select the label

sheet table and remove any before or after spacing. The label sheet table represents the completed merge labels.

Second Issue:

Affecting All Labels Simultaneously:

Scenario:

My labels are generated and positioned up against the left margin. I am using a smaller font and I would like to center the labels a little better within each cell by adjusting the left margin: **Note:** I did not say that I want to center the labels but rather, just want to readjust the left margin a bit.

1.   **Note:** If you highlight all of the labels, and you need to **better position the text** to sit more in the center of the label, all labels will move simultaneously when you adjust the left margin in the ruler. In essence, while the table cells are highlighted, whatever you do in the ruler will affect **all of the addresses simultaneously.** So, if I tug the bottom of the "Hour Glass" (the bottom block) to the right, all of the addresses will move together to the right simultaneously.

By the way, by "Hour Glass", I simply mean the look of the **First Line Indent, The Hanging Indent** and the **Left Margin** when all lined up on top of each other in the ruler.

2.   **Important:** If you wish to make use of the ruler to simultaneously affect all labels at once, then **DO NOT** use the **target symbol** in the upper left hand side of the table to select all the labels. (When in Print Layout View).

3.   Rather, with your cursor in the first cell of your table, just **sweep to the right and down** to highlight your labels.

4.   By doing so, the Hour Glass (left hand side) will **still be visible in the ruler.** If you use the Target symbol to highlight the Labels, the Hour Glass will **disappear from the ruler.**

5.   If you don't care about working with the ruler, then use the Target Symbol to highlight the entire table of labels and go to Paragraph and under **Paragraph** go to "**Left Indent**" and start to adjust the **Left Indent** until you are satisfied with the look.

6.   It should be noted that the Ruler method (tugging the bottom block) will allow you to see the results instantly as you are adjusting (tugging). With the Left Indent method, you will have to come out of the Paragraph Dialog box and see the results and then go back in to readjust if necessary.

Just To Clarify The Spike

The term came up last week from some of our learned operators when I spoke about the use of **Control F3** and **Control Shift F3** in order to cut and paste track changes from one document to another. But although it made use of the spike feature, it was not necessarily the traditional and only way it is used. Some basic facts about this little known feature called the Spike:

1.   We know we have the traditional **clipboard**. The "**Spike**" feature serves to give us a more powerful clipboard by giving it additional functionality.

2.   As we already know, the clipboard (cut or copy) and the spike feature (cut) are meant to compile items that are taken from one location of a document so that they can be pasted somewhere else.

3.   The Spike feature in MS Word lets you to cut and paste non-contiguous text. Non contiguous text means that you can grab let us say five snippets of text and graphics from various areas of a document and have them pasted in their new arrangement in a different area of that same document or another document altogether. Before you make use of the Spike feature, I would duplicate the document that you are going to "**cut**" from. In this way if you need to go back to a pristine copy of the same file you have it.

4.   To send any item to the spike, you can select the piece of text or graphic and press Ctrl+F3 and it will cut the text. The "Spike" feature will allow you to go on sending items to it. Sending a second item to spike will not replace the first item which is what happens when we use the regular clipboard feature.

5.   You can press Press Ctr +Z to restore the removed text (that we threw to the spike clipboard) from the source document if you still need it. ***Ctrl+Z will not remove the text sent to the spike but will simply restore the text you spiked***.

6.   Once you have all the required items in your spike clipboard you can paste it anywhere you need it. Take your cursor where you want to paste the "Spike" clipboard text.

7.   Press Ctrl+Shift+F3 to paste it in.

Fun Fact: You can also type 'spike' where you want to paste the spike and then press F3. This is similar in making use of insert auto text feature.

8. Spike and the Clipboard do not effect each other. If you cut new text (Control X) this won't replace Spike related cuts and an additional new spike (Control F3) won't replace content in the clipboard. So, ***Spike is really a separate storage location than the clipboard***.

9. Remember: Windows clipboard can hold one item at a time. The Office clipboard can hold maximum of 24 items. The "Spike" clipboard can hold thousands of items but *once you insert the Spike cuts that you accumulated and paste them in – the Spike clipboard is then emptied*.

........*

Section Printing

This feature has come to the rescue many a time when the pressure is on, an attorney is standing in the center with you or at your secretarial station, he/she is pacing back and forth and they need a particular piece of a large document right away.

Some of you know exactly what I am referring to. They want a particular piece of the document printed because they need to edit it, they need to go to a meeting with it, they have a conference call due to come in and they just need a particular piece of the whole: What are some of those things that people do and what can you do?

1.   An initial thing people do under pressure is to send the entire document to print. Then they look for the piece that is requested while the attorney looks at them like they are crazy.

2.   Misinterpret the page numbering system within the document 1,2,3 (the page numbering assigned to a particular portion of the document) etc. vs. Page 4 of 120 meaning the "system page count" for that document. This usually results in (over or under printing) pieces or parts of the document that were not requested.

3.   If you are familiar with the document to an extent, then a particular exhibit will have its own section, the main part of the document, will have its own section, the cover page that is vertical aligned center will have its own section, (if you have a cover page) the TOC, TOA, Index of terms depending on the length, will have it own section or individual sections, a portion of the document that has a wide financial table that needed to be placed in the document in landscape will have its own section. Get it?

4.   Knowing this when you go to print, you can select for example Print S5 which means print the 5th section of the document which may be a particular exhibit or Print S3 which may be the main part of the document or S4 which may be that wide financial table so you use this as a way to target a piece within a large file. **S1-S4** will print from the **first** page of Section 1 to the **last** page of Section 4.

Play with this the next time you have a large file. Keep this in the forefront and it will help you to be more efficient in certain situations.

5.   To print a range of pages across sections, use the following:

For example, you would type p1s1-p1s4 to print from page 1 of section 1 through page 1of section 4. Further, to print sections 3 and 5 (but not section 4), type s3,s5.

Remember: The page number and section number are shown in the status bar at the bottom of your screen. If you do not see page number and section number right click on the status bar and turn those features on.

In Word 2013, Word 2010 and in Word 2003, click Print on the File menu.

In Word 2007, click the Microsoft Office Button, and then click Print.

In Word 2013 and 2010, type the range of pages that you want to print in the Pages box in the Settings area.

Finally, In Word 2007 and in Word 2003, click to select the Pages option in the Page range area, and then type the range of pages that you want to print in the box.

........*

Affecting Two Basic Shapes Simultaneously

These are tips that I used many times when dealing with shapes when doing cascading text. But, it does not matter, they are useful for any shapes you are working with.

1.   First, if you need to quickly dupe a shape you can use **Control D**. That will immediately produce a **duplicate** shape. If you are duping the shape for purposes of doing Cascading Text (meaning you are using right triangles) then you are going to need to use the **flip horizontal feature** so that you make sure that the second triangle is facing in towards the first right triangle.

2.   Whether you are using right triangles or not and wish to affect both of the shapes "**simultaneously**" so that making a shape larger, smaller, wider, narrower, the two independent shapes will respond exactly the same if you do the following:

A.   Click on the first shape 1x.

B.   Go to the second shape and do Shift Click.

C.   Now whatever you do will affect **both shapes** simultaneously.

D.   Micro Moving shapes is easy as well. If you need to nudge a shape into place whether it is a text box, (red herring), lines, arrows, ovals etc. you click on the shape and using your **control** and **directional arrow keys** you can **micro move** the object into place. Up, down, left, right. Give it a try!

........*

Some Tips Concerning Email - Survival At Work

I don't have to tell you that when you work for a company, that you have to be aware of certain things relating to using your company email.

1.   Everything you send is saved and most probably monitored at one point or another, so stay away from internal gossip. Not a good idea. If you go to your own email and not the firm issued email, your keystrokes are still being captured on whatever workstation you use or login depending on the size and sophistication of the firm. When you can, use your smart phone to send an email or just wait until you get home. You are better off just staying out of office click situations and their internal email system altogether. Provocative pictures, raunchy jokes and the like when passed around, will show "your email" and "you"

don't know who will be looking at it.   Do you really want to be on the **radar** of Human Resources?

2.   If you are angry about something that either happened in the office or something you received by email, then do your email response as a draft email and do not fill in the recipient line so there is no chance of the email going out prematurely. Wait an hour, look at the response you wrote and remove emotion and anger. Stick to the facts and your suggestions to remedy the situation.

3.   When responding to someone, make sure you select the proper recipient. An example would be you sending an internal email to B. Smith instead of E. Smith. E. Smith never received the email he/she was waiting on from you and now you are home and sleeping.

4.   When sending documents out of the firm, make sure you email the recipient intended. Check the spelling, middle initial etc. Last thing you really want is to send documents to someone that was not supposed to see those particular files.

5.   If you send files to someone with a password, ask the attorney whether the intended party (1) already has the password, (2) If not, will the attorney be the one who calls the client to give them the password? If not, and the recipient is in another time zone and calls for the info to be able to open that file, ask the attorney how late he/she can be called at home. This does happen. Maybe it is Sunday eve where you are, but in China, Japan and Australia, it is late Monday morning and they are doing business and don't want to wait another half a day for you.

6.   Remember to distinguish between link to a file vs. loading up the documents into the email. It is frustrating for a client to have all the files listed but because they are outside your system they cannot access the file(s). Make sure you give them the actual file.

7.   Finally, **slow down**! An extra minute or two won't matter that much but will help to avoid some errors. Read your messages and look for misspellings etc. or missing information. Cc and BC the appropriate people. Focus and things will go smooth.

........*

Open and Repair Can Save The Day:

I was working with an older document in MS Word (not too much older -- MS Word 2003). This document had an area at the very end of the file that would not let the hard return of the last line be on that last line. The hard return was on the next line up against the left margin by itself. I carefully poked around and literally on one character I saw the ruler switch from one long 6.5 inch line to a two column set up as if it were a two column table.

1.   Just in case, I went to columns and made sure under columns that it said one, which it did, so it was not a column problem.

2.   I right clicked on the suspect character and up came those items pertaining to dealing with a table.   But, there was no selection to delete the supposed table and I still could not get the last hard return to pull up.

3:    I also did the customary "**Control Shift N**" in order to attempt to strip whatever might be on that paragraph back to normal but whatever was invisible to me was still in there even in Normal.

4.   Finally, I closed the document and went to File Open and located the file on the hard drive. I clicked on the file name 1X, and directly next to the OPEN button, I clicked on the down arrow and selected Open and Repair.

5.   When it opened up, it cleaned out the problem and the document was fine. Open and Repair is a great tool. Even if you have a DMS system (Document Management System), you can download the file to your hard drive, run the Open and Repair and then replace the DMS bad version of that document with the newly fixed document that you just ran the Open and Repair on.

6.   Remember, you must be in MS Word and go to the file by File Open. *You cannot use* **Open and Repair** *if you access the file by going to Explore meaning right clicking on your start button and navigating to the file by that method.* It works the majority of the time on quirky documents and can be a great tool for situations that seem to be problems in the Visual Basic and therefore not apparent to the operator.

Alertness and Routines Solve Problems and Catch Errors

I just got finished looking at George's (one of my students) write up named "**Text Boxes/Pictures not printing**". In this article, he alerts us to something that might have made many people in the group waste a lot of time until they centered on the problem. It was a simple thing being Options/Display/Printing Options and an unchecked box called "**Print drawings created in Word**". The word Drawings would have thrown me off. Things like this make a difference in our library of situations that we have experienced.

In talking further about Detail. I have seen the following scenario unfold numerous times and this article will put this particular situation in the back of your head as well and will help to underscore the importance of an established routine.

Scenario: Attorney brings down document. He says: Dupe the document and make the heavy markup changes under the new document number. Do not touch original document.

1.   Operator dupes document. He writes the new number on his log sheet while he is in the process of filling out the document summary.

2.   What the operator does not realize is that the footer did not update properly from the DMS and the new document is still displaying the original file number in the footer.

3.   He goes directly into the new file and after doing about 5 pages of heavy edits he places a pickup sheet telling the next operator where to continue the edits.

4.   As most operators do, they pick of the mark-up, look at the footer and go into the document whereupon they continue the editing in the original file. He finishes the file, prints it out and sends it back to the attorney.

5.   The attorney receives a document that he asked not to be edited, heavily edited and the first five pages of the new document being done properly have not yet come to the attention of the attorney. It will be up to a confused coordinator and the original operator to finally figure out what happened here. This is a mess and could have been totally been avoided if the operator simply checked the new file to make sure the footer updated. Small routines such as checking the footer go a long way.

........*

Cutting Down On The Amount of Electronic Theft

I do a lot of producing of my own books and materials for business consulting and I have to be aware of materials being outright lifted and my hard work being passed around at my expense.

I have also produced materials (reports, industry research etc.) for law firms in the WP center that were researched and written by attorneys on behalf of a client that wanted to be assured that their materials were not easily reproduced and if passed around, wanted to be assured that their company info and watermark was not ever removed.

Now, some of you will say what can you do? You can do plenty and I am going to show you.

1.   Let us start out by saving your MS Word Document as a PDF.

2.   Depending on where you work, some of you will have Adobe Professional and some of you will be using Nuance for your PDF creation and other related procedures. For

the sake of all being on the same page, I will refer to the Adobe software. Nuance is very similar and a good product.

3.	Now, the attorney will have let you know what he/she wants in the watermark. Place the watermark on the page "Diagonally" and make it large enough and dark enough with the "transparency" feature but light enough where it does not become overly intrusive. After all, you need to be able to read the text.

4.	Two things to consider. If you place a password on the PDF file to allow only printing and no editing, there are too many programs that will break an Adobe password. Look it up and you find page after page. If you place the Watermark in the MS Word file and then PDF the file, they will simply in Adobe Professional, go to **Tools, Advanced Tools** and **Touch Up Object** where they will be able to get direct access to the layer the watermark sits in and will simply delete it and they are home free.

5.	So, knowing this, take your PDF file and save the entire file as JPG's. Going back to Adobe Professional, I create a new PDF "based on the multiple files" option. Select all the JPGs and Adobe will compile them into a new Adobe file.

6.	This will ensure that the watermark is now intertwined with the text (no longer on a separate layer) and can not be removed nor the text scanned without it being an absolute mess. Most of the people who take other people's work don't really want to retype anything. If it is not easy, then they are likely not to go the extra mile. Yes, there might be some loss of clarity but changing the Font in the MS Word File will produce different results in this process. The simpler the font the less blurring you will have.

If you are producing material, you have to take steps to protect your work whether it is your personal project or for the law firm. We are in an era where free to most people means valueless, and too many people will attempt to take if they can. What we want to do is to make it a bit harder. This is a valuable process to know so go through a mock document to get the routine down.

........*

Oh No - It happened Again

I actually covered this before to some extent in an article I did called "**X Marks the Spot**" in Volume 1, but I came across the problem again on a forum and it played out as an unnecessary comedy of errors. In fact, the person from the forum got a lot of unnecessary attention for putting a few high end printers out of commission and it impacted his temp job.

So here it is again with a little twist:

Problem: We are about to print 200 2x4 labels. We load 20 label sheets into the printer tray. After sending them to print, we go over to the printer to pick them up and they are printed on the wrong side.

1.   Now, I can tell you that I have personally watched many a person dump them in the garbage at this point. But this person, in this scenario, said hey, I will just turn them over and put them through again.

2.   Okay, so he turns them over and sends them to print and this time they print on the proper side meaning the labels, but, upon examining the label sheets he notices that on some of the sheets labels are missing.

3.   Where did they go? They are glued and melted on the burning hot roller in the printer. Now running regular documents through that printer results in remnants of glue and label adhering to letters and other legal documents thus making that printer sort of useless until someone scrapes everything off including the molten glue from the labels or in some cases, a service call has to be made in order to replace the roller so that it can be cleaned professionally.

4.   So, how do we avoid this scenario? If you should make the initial error (and it is a common error) of putting the labels through on the wrong side, don't use that same printer since it will be burning hot! If you want to run them through again, let the label sheets cool for about 10 minutes and go to a **cold printer** meaning one that has not just been used. In this way, you can salvage the labels and they are unlikely to come off of the sheets.

This comes up from time to time, but, now you will know how to handle this situation at work.

........*

The 3 Essentials When Doing Cleanup

I have been doing a lot of clean-up as of late. Part of the cleanup involves.

1.   Changing the font for the document as a whole.

2.   Making sure the margins are 1 inch all around.

3.   Making sure section breaks are set for **New Page** and **Different First Page** applied to the entire document.

4.   Making sure that the document is set for **top alignment** with the exception of the **Cover Page** which I set for **Vertical Alignment Center**.

Now even though you have switched the font for the entire document, there can be areas of the text where fonts were applied to pieces of text by direct formatting. This is why you will still see mixtures of fonts within the text after you have changed the document font.

As part of the cleanup routine, I select all the text (Control A) and then do Control Spacebar which strips off any fonts that were directly applied so that only the font selected for the document as a whole remains.

So, below is a nice summary of what I call the 3 essentials that you should make full use of as needed.

CTRL+ SPACE – This removes all character-level formatting—strange fonts, underlining, boldface, italics, etc. Just select the text you want to fix and hit this key combination (hold down your Control key and press the space bar).

CTRL+ Q – This removes all paragraph-level formatting—out of place indents, line spacing, extra spacing before and after the paragraphs, etc. Again, select the text, hold down your Control key and press the letter Q.

CTRL+ SHIFT +N – This returns the selected text to Normal formatting (however Normal is defined in that particular document's Styles).

........*

Clarifying The Use Of The Style Separator

I write this short article just to clarify when to make use of the style separator.

Basics:

The style separator is used when a Heading Level that is going to be included in a Table of Contents (TOC) **shares the paragraph** with body text **instead of** being on its **own line.**

In order to let MS Word know where the heading text ends and the body text of the shared paragraph begins, we use the style separator (**control alt enter**) after the Heading Text which acts as a cut off.

What I observe is the following:

1.   Use of style separator on paragraphs that look like the following.

(a)   Body Text Body Text Body Text Body Text Body Text Body Text Body Text

(i)   Body Text Body Text Body Text Body Text Body Text Body Text Body Text

(•)   Body Text Body Text Body Text Body Text Body Text Body Text Body Text

2.	These type of Headings (usually Heading 3 and 4) will **not be** in the TOC but if they were, the Headings would surely have Heading Text and **not just a letter bullet or number**.

3.	Finally, "if" a particular Heading shares the paragraph but is "not" going to be used in the TOC (such as a level 3 or 4) then again, you do not need to use the style separator. If the attorney at some point asks for the level 3 or levels 3 and 4 to be included then you should use (include) the Style Separator for those levels.

4.	Using style separator is a lot easier than the old style of using returns with the "Hidden" attribute applied to them in order to separate the heading text from the body text. Most often, they would color the hidden returns Red to alert operators of its use but still many an operator or secretary not understanding what was going on would routinely remove the returns and we would be back to square one.

5.	For those of you who do not have third party software to take care of the Style Separator situation, it does a very good job when applied correctly.

6.	For convenience, throw the Style Separator icon ¶¶ on your Quick Access Toolbar for those of you that do not like the control keys. You will find it under **All Commands** under File – Options – Quick Access Toolbar.

........*

Dealing With Linked Styles

Until 2007, we had two types of styles sitting in the style task pane on the right side of your page.

1.	Those with the paragraph symbol to the right of the style name are styles that affect the entire paragraph when applied.

### Article Heading	¶

2.	Those styles with a small "a" underscored to the right of the style name refer to **Character Styles** which are meant to affect only a portion of text by placing an attribute on that text such as a font, bold, italic, underscore etc.. The character styles **do not** get tracked in the style area pane on the left side when in Draft View but simply co-exist within a paragraph style when applied.

Page Number	a

3.	Now we also have what are referred to as **Linked Styles**:

Linked Styles are a combination of both **paragraph** and **character styles**. In the style task pane on the right side of your screen, a Linked Style will have a paragraph and character style symbol together to the right of the style name. This is how a Linked Style works.

Body Text 2   ¶a

4.   A linked style behaves as either a character style or a paragraph style, depending on what you select. If you click in a paragraph or select a paragraph and then apply a linked style, the style is applied as a paragraph style. However, if you select (highlight) a word or phrase in the paragraph and then apply a linked style, the style is applied as a character style, with no effect on the paragraph as a whole.

5.   For example, if you select (or click in) a paragraph and then apply the Heading 1 style, the whole paragraph is formatted with the Heading 1 text and paragraph characteristics.

6.   However, if you select a word or a phrase and then apply Heading 1, the text that you selected is formatted with the text characteristics of the Heading 1 style, but none of the paragraph characteristics are applied

To disable linked styles:

ALT + CTRL + SHIFT + S to open the 'styles' list. Select the 'Disable Linked Styles' check box.

........*

Using Indent Vs. Using The Target Symbol - There Is A Difference

What is this about? Let's say preference and functionality.

We are talking about finished labels. When you run a merge or place labels on a sheet let us say 2x4 size, they have a tendency to come in to the left of the label thus leaving **a lot of empty space** to the right on each label.

People generally want to center the address of each label so it is nice and balanced on the label. Centering for purposes of this discussion should be thought of in 1 of 2 ways. One way is to literally center each individual label by use of the center icon or Control E.

Some people do not like the look of the label when each individual line of the address is centered. Instead, they like to adjust the left margin and push it so to speak to the center of the label while keeping the left aligned look of the label.

Left Indent

Mr. Joe Smith
Anywhere Street
Anyway, USA 11345

vs.

Centered Address

Mr. Joe Smith
Anywhere Street
Anyway, USA 11345

This is the essence of what I want to talk about. The two ways in which we can adjust the left margin in order to better center each address in the individual labels on the sheet.

1.   Try this first. Make sure your ruler is on. Sweep across and highlight the first 6 labels. By sweeping across the labels rather than selecting the "target symbol" that comes up on the left side of the table when in Print Layout View, your ruler will be visible and so will the hour glass looking figure on the left side of your ruler.

2.   By hour glass figure, I am referring to the First Line Indent, Hanging Indent and Left Margin when all lined up on top of each other. Anyway, when you sweep across the labels and highlight them in that way, you can go to the bottom block of the hour glass on the ruler and tug it toward the right and all the highlighted labels will react uniformly at once and this is very visual in terms of lining something up in this case, centering address info comfortably on each label.

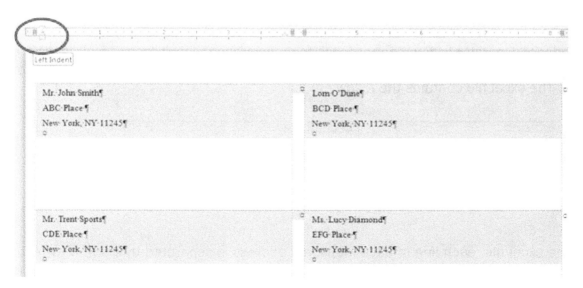

3.   The other method to center the labels but keep the left aligned aspect is to use the target symbol on the top left of the table which will select the entire table at once. Your ruler will now disappear.

4.   Go to Paragraph and go to Left Indent and place a figure in such as 1.0 and see how the labels respond meaning how they sit within each individual label.

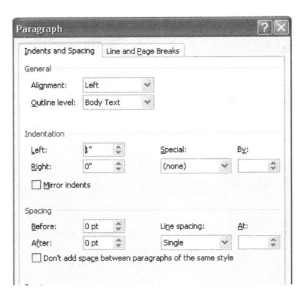

5.   If the info is nicely centered on the label then great. If not, with the entire table selected, adjust the left indent setting by increasing or decreasing the indentation setting until the labels sit nicely centered.   Get comfortable with both methods of adjusting the left margin.

........*

Problem Relating To Data Info In Excel File Re Merge

Scenario: Operator is given a merge file to do whereby the names and addresses are sitting in an excel file.   They want the Excel file to be used as the name and address file for the Merge. The excel file contains the following:

Name and Address¤	Salutation¤
Mr. Joe Smith↵ 123 Anywhere Street↵ New York, NY 10019¤	Mr. Smith¤

In the excel file, each line of each individual address is separated by a soft return (alt enter). When the merge is run however, there is a hard return at the end of each line of the inside address and 12 PTS after in the resulting MS Word Output Merge File which is a problem and looks like the sample below:

Mr. Joe Smith (hard return)

12 points of space

123 Anywhere Street (hard return)

12 points of space

New York, NY 10019 (hard return)

12 points of space

1.   Unlike using soft returns in a MS Word Name and Address portion of a Merge Data File, the soft returns used in the same portion of the Excel file had no positive effect on the resulting Merge Output File whereby we end up with a hard return at the end of each line of the inside address.

2   In the Merge Letter itself on the line containing the Merge Field Code for the Name and Address Info, we establish a style (call it inside address) that does not have any after spacing. Therefore, when the merge is run, the hard return sitting at the end of each line of the return address lines from the resulting Excel file no longer produces the extra space between each line.

3.   The trick is whatever follows the inside address such as a Re: Line or a Salutation line. make sure you build **12 PTS Before** spacing into **that style that controls the Re Line or Salutation** since we took the 12 PTS After Spacing out of the Inside Address Style.

4.   This article was written so that you will be aware of certain considerations that crop up when Excel is used to hold the Name and Address information that will be used in the merge.

........*

If More Than One Page Do The Following

We are talking about the TOC, TOA and Index of Terms.

On short documents, the Table of Contents, Table of Authorities and Index of Terms can be separated by a page break. The Table of Contents heading and the other headings are centered horizontally on the actual page not in the Header. The page numbering type is i, ii, ii,

Table of Contents

-----Page Break

Table of Authorities

-----Page Break

Index of Terms

-----Section Break

First Page of Actual Document

For long documents, you just might have a Table of Contents or Table of Authorities, that exceed one page and you need to deal with them differently:

1.   Between the TOC, TOA and Index there should be a section break

2.   In the first page header of the TOC page do the following:

3.   Go into the header and type:

Table·of·Contents¶

4.   On the second page header of the completed and generated TOC page type in:

Table·of·Contents¶
(continued)¶

5.   Do the same routine for the TOA and Index if needed.

6.   Make sure you remember to **turn off** Link To Previous **as you set these up** so that your Headings don't jump into sections that were not meant to have those headings.

........*

Keep With Next - Every Document Is A Bit Different:

The **Keep With Next, Keep Lines Together** and **Page Break Before** are part of the Paragraph Dialog Box under and Line and Page Breaks. You know when it is being used because of the Tell-Tale little black box that sits to the extreme left of each paragraph where it is in use.

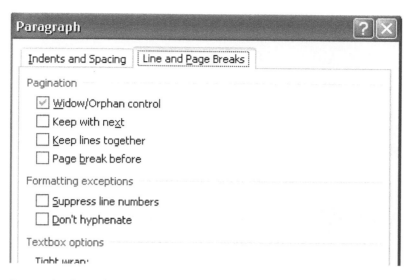

Its main function is to deal with **headings** and **beginnings of paragraphs** that are left at the **bottom** of a page while the paragraph associated with that Heading or the remainder of a paragraph **fall to the next page**. The feature makes sure that the Heading and the paragraph that follows stays together.

This article is essentially about "Keep With Next" and avoiding unintentional overuse.

Normally, we "tend" to build Keep With Next into Level 1 and 2 at the most of a Multi-Level Outline. The problems occur when:

1)   Keep With Next Is Built Into Levels 3, 4 and beyond which then disturbs the natural breaking of the pages.

2)   We use **Keep With Next** on a level such as Level Heading 2 that happens to make up the majority of the paragraphs in the document. This then results in the same problem of not allowing the document to break naturally and pages are unusually short in many places throughout the document.

What should we do as a practice when dealing with Keep With Next?

1.   Take a look at each document that is 10 pages and above and look to see what styles and/or levels of a Multi-Level Outline Keep With Next is being utilized on.

2.   If Levels Headings 1 and 2 have it built-in, you can leave it providing the level Heading 2 is not making up the majority of the paragraphs in the document.

3.   If you come across paragraphs (Multi-Level or Not) that need **Keep With Next protection**, then simply go to **Paragraph under the Home Tab**

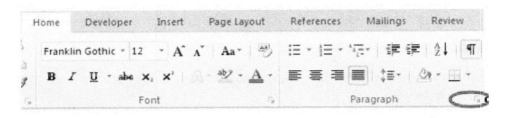

and go to **Line and Page Breaks** and select Keep With Next.

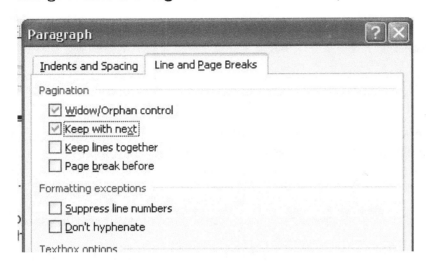

The use of **Keep With Next** in this manner is considered **Direct Formatting** but it is perfectly acceptable. Many uses of Keep With Next are performed on an as needed basis and not built into the style.

Get familiar with using the **Line and Page Breaks Dialog Box** and you will develop a good handle on when to make use of the selections available as you are doing your documents.

........*

Two Document Numbers In The Footer - One Is Enough

This scenario usually occurs when one is using a **Document Management System** ("DMS") such as **Docs Open** or **iManage** and they were told to **Dupe** a particular document.

When you copy a document, many firms use a macro that places the new Document Number in the Footer of the new document thus replacing the old number.

Sometimes, it does not replace the old number due to the original number being out of its usual position or having been typed in manually. Either way, a minor thing like this can cause a major problem. Let me explain how:

1.   Let us say we don't correct this. They told you to dupe the document and make the edits in a version 2 of the newer document.

2.   You place your new document number on your Document Log Sheet and you print out the document and package it up for the next operator to pick up where you left off.

3.   The next operator comes in and sees your note where to pick up with the edits and takes a glance at the hard copy and goes into the first number he sees on the bottom of the document. He doesn't realize that he just went back to the original document where he continues to edit from the pick-up point left by the first operator.

4.   You can see the potential for a mess. When creating a new document or duping a document, always check that the new document number has made it to the footer of the new document and HAS REPLACED THE OLD (ORIGINAL NUMBER).

5.   Also, make sure that the new document number has totally replaced the former number all the way through the document. Place your new document number on your personal document log of the day and make sure that when leaving a document to be continued by another operator that you **always mention the new document number** that you wish the next operator to go into. Clarity in terms of the document number involved and what is being asked will ensure a smooth turnover.

........*

It's Okay, Don't Touch

This particular article has to do with Multilevel Outlining.

Any of my students know that I look at each level (Heading Level) of a Multi-Level Outline in two ways. I first deal with the Numbering Aspect of a particular level and then the Textual Aspect.

Article 1. (Numbering Aspect)

Introduction (Textual Aspect)

Section 1.1 (NA) - Method of Operation (TA) Anyway, when we position the Numbering to where we want it to line up, we make use of the "**Aligned at**" and "**Indent at**" part of the **Multilevel Dialog Box**.

The problem that students and operators alike encounter is the claim that nothing has taken effect. Meaning that the settings they placed in the Multi-Level dialog box will not take effect.

Here are two common reasons why:

1   The Level 3 in the Multi-Level Dialog Box is not Linked to Heading 3.

Or

2.   When the operator takes care of the Textual portion of the particular Heading Style, they go into for example Heading 2 (under Modify) Format Paragraph and take care of things such as line spacing and Before and After spacing.

3.   What they should NOT be touching is **Left Indent** and anything under Special namely, **First Line Indent**.

The settings that one sees when dealing with a live Multi-Level outline when going into **Format Paragraph** when modifying a Heading Style in terms of **Indent** and under **Special** are settings **reflecting the choices** that "**were made**" when setting the position of the numbering aspect when you were in the Multi-Level Dialog box.

4.   When people see settings in the paragraph dialog box that they themselves did not put in, they tend to want to remove them **not making the connection** that those settings are simply stemming from what they just set in the Multi-Level Dialog box.

So, as I said, it's okay don't touch

........*

Very Simple, But You Can Get Momentarily Confused

I like to include these quick fixes because minor problems are amplified when a person in a law firm setting is under stress, time constraint, and/or an attorney is present and is demanding a document to be completed or fixed.

So here is the scenario:

Document has a large table mostly consisting of text that extends over 20 pages. It has a large textual header row. The Header Row repeats on each page because "**Header Row Repeat**" has been selected.

The operator is complaining about a certain area in the document they need to edit but cannot click upon to position the cursor. They have already spent too much time looking at the table thinking someone has locked that part of the document from being able to be edited.

What actually happened is the following:

1.   The attorney, 10 pages into the hard copy, made edits to the large repeated table heading at the top of page 10.

2.   The operator, on page 10 of the document, was trying to edit the area that the attorney made edits to on the hard copy to no avail.

3.   The operator was then directed to go back to page 1 of the table and to edit the header from that location. The hard copy momentarily confused the operator because the attorney did not realize that the repetitive header info is un-editable unless of course you go back to **Row 1** of the table where the Table Header originated.

4.   The operator went back to row 1 and made the changes then, went back to page 10 and continued on with the edits for the remainder of the document.

Simple, but then again, it is always simple when you have already been there.

........*

Separating Out An MS Word Output Merge File

Scenario as described in this article: 2 Page Letter going to 150 separate people.

Output file thus produces a 300 page file with 150 section breaks.

There is a macro that will separate out each individual output letter to a new file.

Personally, I would probably just use two trays if I had to use letter head or just print out the entire 300 page file. I would then collate and separate the letters.

But when there are agreements being used for the merge and let us say that there are 10 agreements generated, it will sometime make sense to separate them into separate output files. The following link will take you to a macro that does just that.

If you look in Microsoft's Knowledge Base, you will find that there is an old article that deals with this very issue:

http://support.microsoft.com/kb/216201

The macro presented in the article, even though it was written for Word 97, will work just fine in Word 2007 and later versions. It allows you to separate a merged document into individual files, based on the section breaks:

http://wordribbon.tips.net/T008435_Merging_to_Individual_Files.html
........*

Two Methods of Submitting Inserts In Large Documents:

No doubt, if you work in a law firm for any length of time, you know that the documents you receive can be a road map of inserts or an intertwined jungle of text and hard to read handwriting going vertically, on the page and continuing onto the back of the page.

There is not much you can do with the senior attorney who will take exception to your suggestions on how to structure the inserts but you may have some luck with the newer associates who may be open to the old "Letter Style" insert method.

So, for large inserts (over a paragraph) you assign a letter "A" to the first insert and the attorney then either types up the text or hand writes the **Insert A** text on a separate sheet of paper or if typing a separate document. On the hard copy of the attorney Mark-up, the attorney would just place an "A" at the location where the insert is to be inserted. He/She then repeats this process for all of the inserts.

If the attorney is willing to do this method, this will certainly cut down on mistakes and improve accuracy when keying in the inserts.

If you as a secretary or WP center person would write up a "suggested method" (a one pager) with visual example for dealing with inserts, then it is possible that it will be adopted by the attorneys. If they see the merit of doing inserts in this way, cutting down on errors and improving the turnaround time, there is hope that they may be open to adopting this long standing method.

Then there are attorneys who bring down inserts that are actually paragraphs within other already existing documents and they give you the document numbers where you can copy the text. You of course would then bring the text into the target document using Paste Special. Those attorneys already understand the **"A" to "A"** concept and would be a good candidate.

If you have any other suggestions for dealing with inserts and heavy Mark-up feel free to share your tips.

........*

Search and Replace With The Choice to Go No Further.

Experienced WP operators and Secretaries who make use of the following featured scenario be aware to "be aware". A great feature that can do some damage.

What is this about? There are situations where you want to use search and replace to take care of something that may not be for the entire document but for a selected (highlighted) piece of text. **I'll give you a few examples**:

1.   You have 10 lines in a particular paragraph with a of (I), (II), (III) type numbering system throughout the 10 lines and you want to quickly protect that particular paragraph with non breaking spaces after each closed parenthesis.

2.   You have multiple areas in a document that look like inside addresses, multiple line letterheads or multiple line Titles where you want to make use of soft returns instead of hard returns with the exception of the last line.

3.   Finally, you have an area of text that says "for a period of 20 days" numerous times in a particular paragraph and you need to switch that over to 25 days.

So, we highlight the piece or area of text that we wish to affect with our global replace. I like to use the **Control H** shortcut.

1.   When you run the global replace, it will do the replace on the text you highlighted and will then give you a message that it has made X number of replacements

and asks you if you wish to now run it for the remainder of the document and to that you say "**NO**"

2.   If you are not paying attention and you say yes, then depending on what you set the search up to do, you may do a lot of damage to a large document and you **May Not Even Notice!**

3.   If it were a small document, you most probably would notice this and take action to "**Undo**" the problem. In a large file, this type of error could be replicated 100's of times and barely noticed. Then, you go ahead and save your document not knowing there is now major problems from a global replace that was meant to only affect a small portion of the document. You then give it back to Mr. or Ms. Attorney and what a shock when they start to examine their document.

4.   In sum, when you run a global replace that involves the highlighting of a selected portion of text, be alert, run the global and when it stops to ask you whether you want to run it for the remainder of the document say NO.

5.   Potential problems are totally avoidable by just being alert. Also, we can't be certain that we can fix the document quickly or get our hands on a pristine copy before the occurrence happened so be alert.

........*

The Organizer

While this article will speak about the Organizer, I want to discuss why you would need to use it.

Depending on the type of firm and how tight the control is at that firm, you (1) may be able to develop a template. (2) may not be allowed to develop anything without the permission of the IT Dept., (3) encouraged to create styles as needed, (4) discouraged from making additional styles. Whatever the situation, as long as you can get to the organizer you can shortcut a lot of the grunt work as per creating styles that fit a particular document type.

I recently had to reformat a set of documents that only slightly differed but in terms of formatting, they were essentially the same. So I have four things that I could do as it relates to grabbing a set of styles.

1.   I could use Control Shift C and Control Shift V to Copy a style from one document to another one by one.

2.   I could create a template and have all of these pre-made styles ready but I may not be willing to yank the text out of the existing document and into the template.

3.   I could add all of these helpful styles into the Normal dotm file but depending on where you work they may not want the Normal Dot modified (**added to or removed from**)

4.   Finally, I could open the Organizer, and on the **left side** have open the document that **needs the styles** and on the **right side**, have open the document that **contains all of the great styles** that you put together for a particular document type. Copy them over to the left side and you are good to go.

So, how do we get to the Organizer?

1   Go To The Home Tab.

2.   Turn on your right side Style Panel

3.   Go To The Bottom and choose "**Manage Styles**"

4.   Choose "**Import/Export**".

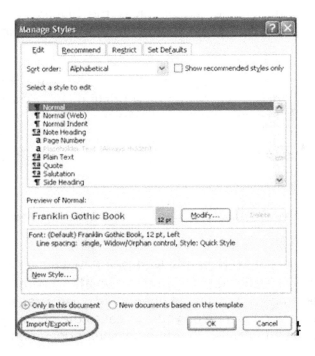

5.   Your Organizer will come up initially showing the Normal.dotm file on the right side and the current open document will be represented on the left side.

6.   If you are in Draft View, you can also **double click** on the **Left Side Style Tracking Area** and when "**Modify**" comes up, on the lower left hand portion you will see the **Organizer Button**.

7.	Open up the desired file instead of the Normal.dotm (meaning close the Normal.dotm and open up the document that has the styles you need) and proceed to copy what you need over to the left side. Once you do, those styles will now be available in the document you are currently working in.

This is a feature you should know about and all of the advantages this gives you in terms of not having to reinvent the wheel over and over again.

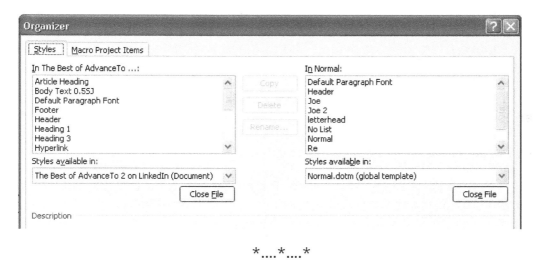

........*

Save Your Eyes When Doing Your Work On Screen and Off

What I am writing in this article, I have to remind myself to do on a continuous basis.

1.	Hard Copy: (Paper). Example: You receive a heavy markup with a very thick set of edits. The handwriting is both small and poor. How many people including myself have I seen struggling just to make out the words let alone there are 80 pages of this mess.

Before you struggle, make your life easier by going to your copier and copy the markup to 110% which will make it much easier to see what is going on.

2.   You are doing a mark-up and you find yourself squinting while looking at the screen. The zoom on the bottom right is right there for you to access. If you have a heavy markup whereby you need to carefully look at the markup and then relocate your eyes to where a "specific edit" is to be made, then zoom it up to around 115-120% and that will make a major difference in your day. No need for you to strain your eyes trying to zone in on where you have to make an edit. I know it seems obvious but I have seen enough people struggle unnecessarily.

3.   Do remember that if you bump up your view to assist your editing, then before you send your document to a client or back to the attorney, remember to take it back to 100% and save it so that the recipient sees the usual look when they open the file.

For those of you that are doing 8 and 12 hour shifts, just doing what I have discussed will help to prevent eye fatigue and your editing will be more accurate.

........*

Use Your Views To Avoid Misinterpreting What You See

You will see why I chose this title.

This week, I watched an operator while in Draft View remove continuous section breaks thinking they were a mistake. He did this for about 10 pages before it came to the attention of the attorney.

1.   I love Draft View because I like to make use of the Style Tracking on the left hand side and the ability to double click on the left hand side style names to modify a style.

2.   Back to the issue. When in **Draft** view, anything using Columns (not tables) will appear as one long strip of text. It is not until you switch over to **Print Layout View** that you will see the intended look meaning newspaper like columns or blog like columns or text reproduced in columns to cut down on the length of a document etc.

3.   You won't see your **Text Box** or **Page Borders** when you are in **Draft View** but you will see your **Text Box** and **Page Borders** when in **Print Layout View**.

4.   If you come across something that at first glance looks like "junk" before you delete it switch your view and make sure you see the whole picture.

5.   Another quick example: Before Style Separator, we used the hidden attribute on the return symbol and made the return symbol Red. People coming along and deleting all the Red Returns (Pilcros) and thus removing the Style Separator option at that time was a very common occurrence. If they would have poked around just a bit, they would have realized that the returns marked as hidden and colored Red was not an error but an important part of that particular document.

In sum, take another look before you undo something that you feel may be an error. It just may have a perfectly good reason behind it.

If You Happen To Work In A WP Center then It Is Good To Know These Tools

The gentlemen who wrote the article that I reference here (Geoff Ronning), is a specialist on creating video seminars. He wrote the article from the perspective of a marketing person analyzing his competitors. He is very good at what he does and always shares a lot of good info. Even though he is not a Word Processing person, he covers material that we are asked to do from time to time. Because it is from time to time, we don't always remember the solution right away. This article should be filed under Websites-Video-Audio. This article provides a number of quick solutions:

In this article you will learn some of the following:

1.   How to capture intact an entire webpage.

2.   Download videos from webpages.

3.   Download You Tube Videos.

4.   Convert Video to alternative formats.

5.   What are the best screen recorders

6.   Convert video to audio.

7.   Access a particular website's SEO info to see how they were able to position themselves to the top.

8.   What tools did the target website use.

http://geoffronning.com/sneaky-competitor-research-tools/?utm_campaign=weekly-2015_11_3&utm_medium=email&utm_source=newsletter

........*

Dealing With Footnote Separator Lines

This is a minor item but it can get you into trouble if you are under pressure.

Scenario:

You are dealing with Footnotes that are long. Because of their length, the other aspects of the Footnote function kick in namely **Footnote Continuation Separator** and **Footnote Continuation Notice**.

Let's say the attorney wants you to alter the Footnote Continuation Separator Line. Instead of the line going all the way across, they have requested for it to go 3/4 as a preferred look and I have personally been asked to have the line match the initial short line all the way through the document as well as the spillover pages where Footnotes were too big to fit on the bottom of the page. This means you have to be able to get to the line to edit it.

The Key thing to remember is **Draft View**. You cannot get to the Separator Lines for editing purposes from Print Layout View and not knowing this can cause major problems and frustration. I have seen many a person frustrated that they cannot get to edit the line nor get to the footnote text. The menus are a bit different but even in 2003 back to MS Word 97 you had to be in **Draft View** that was the former "**Normal**" view in order to have access. So with this being said, let's see how you would edit the separator lines.

1.   Go to Draft View

2.   Go to References

3.   Choose Show Notes

4.   At the bottom of the screen Click on down arrow next to Footnote Separator Line

5.   Now you can select:

A.   Footnote separator (where you can add before or after spacing)

B.   Footnote continuation Separator (where you can alter the line length or add before or after spacing)

C.   Footnote continuation notice (where you can add before or after spacing and change the notice as you see fit).

D.   If you need to modify the **Footnote Reference Number,** you would modify the style **Footnote Ref** while needing to modify the Footnote text you would modify the style **Footnote Text.**

I would strongly suggest that you create a footnote and go through the process of editing this area if needed. In this way, you have already gone through the process and you are not caught off guard.

........*

Doc Comparison- Not only for comparing two in-house documents

Whether you are using MS Word's Document Comparison feature (under the Review Tab) or a third party Document Comparison software such as Work Share (Deltaview), we tend to use it for in-house use.

We routinely use it in order to show the progress between two versions of a document that the attorneys are working on.

We don't always use it fully to our advantage. Let me explain:

Example: The firm sends a contract on behalf of a client to a customer of the client to be printed and signed so that an agreement can be concluded for some business deal.

You receive back an electronic or paper copy that has been signed. Many times, I have observed that when they get the contract back, they don't typically run a comparison to see that nothing has been altered. I have personally witnessed the alteration of an NDA (Non-Disclosure-Agreement), where the "In Force and Effect" section **kept being changed** to 1 year instead of 2 years. It may be a small change, but to the entity that wanted to keep something under wraps, the other side sneakily shaved off a year. That is not something you want to overlook and it tells a lot about that group of people. If you don't check the document coming back against the document you sent out, you won't necessarily know that an "unauthorized" change has been made.

If you send out a PDF of the contract you can still run a comparison whether you are using Adobe Professional or Nuance. You can also password protect the PDF to prevent any changes to the document. Therefore they need to print it, sign-it and rescan it as well as sending back a signed hard copy if requested.

Unless you send someone a contract where a courier waits for the party to sign the document and hand it back to the courier, you should run a comparison if possible. In a larger contract, if someone should alter the language just a bit, that alteration could have a significant effect on the meaning or terms within.

It is a good habit to run document compares on **ANY** documentation that was supposed to be "Post" editing or development. It is a good way to spot even the slightest alteration.

........*

Matching The Color Of A Photo May Be Easier Than You Think

Scenario: A Cover Page For A Report. Background black. Decent size photo: Dusk sky (mixture of blue, white, light grey) and a nice picture of a bridge over the water. Nice night time like scene. The task asked was to make a border on the page (**top, bottom, left, right**) using text boxes (width 0.5) which matched the same color combo as the dusk sky.

1.   Using the color mixing aspect concerning the "Fill of the text box", I just could not match the sky. It sort of looked like it but, a cheap cartoon version of it and it did not work visually.

2.   So, resorting to an old trick, I am going to use Snag-it (you can use any software that lets you capture an area of the screen).

3.   I go over to the area of the picture that has the color mixture of the sky that they needed and I captured that area which was a perfect representation of the blend they were looking for and saved it as a JPG.

4.   I now went to each separate text box and using the "picture fill" loaded up the JPG and thus perfectly matched the blend they were seeking.

5.   It is an old method, but when needed, it always works and can save you a lot of time and effort.

........*

Field Shading On Word Fillable Forms - On or Off

On doing fillable forms, using MS Word 2007-13, (under the Developer Tab), you have a choice of using the old style fillable forms (Legacy)

or the newer version which is known as (Content Control).

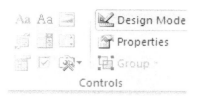

Controls

Sometimes we use a hybrid of both the new fillable forms and the old in the same document. More often it is one or the other. Most people don't care if the grey shading of the Legacy forms are visible on the text fields of the form while others want it off. It should also be noted that from document to document, I have seen the setting we are about to discuss both on and off so you have to check.

This particular article deals with the Legacy text field. Here is the situation. Some people want the grey fields to be visible when the form is used and some want nothing to show but rather, want to rely on the tab key to just bounce them from one field to another within the form. So, the question becomes what controls whether the grey field shows up when using text form fields?

1.   Grey shading "Always" under File Properties, Advanced **DOES NOT** control this.

2.   Use of the highlighter **DOES NOT** control this.

3.   Under your **Developer Tab**, go to the **Legacy Forms Tool Box** (looks like a **Yellow** folder)

4.   Go to the " second from end of first line (within the Legacy Forms tool box) and click it off to turn it off and keep it on to see the grey field if they do not want the form field visible when the recipient receives and uses the form. But, since the Grey shading does not print, I do not agree to turn it off. I believe that it should always be on.

5.   When creating your form with the grey shading off, you will still see the tell tale circles "ooooo" but when the form is locked down the recipient will not.

6.   It should be noted that although the grey field is off, as someone tabs through the file and hits each field area, the field will become blue. When the grey shading is on the field area will look like this:

I have authored a great book on Fillable Forms. If you go to **www.lowcostempire.com** and **MS. Word Business Books**, you will find my book (**Low Cost Empire Volume 10**) that thoroughly goes over both the Legacy and the Content Control Fillable Forms. A great book and a great value.

........*

Inserting Sound Files Into Your MS Word File:

I worked with an attorney on a weekend shift who was working hard on a brief. Many areas of the brief still needed to be researched and composed by Associates assigned to the project.

He (the Partner) went through the document and at specific locations he quickly laid out his thoughts and possible strategies as a series of audio files instead of typing a ton of comments. He felt it was much easier for him than excessive typing since the document had a lot of issues that were up in the air. He felt it was a more effective way to relay his thoughts. So, the question becomes, how do we embed audio files in the MS Word Document.

1. Position the insertion point where you want the sound inserted.

2. Display the Insert tab of the ribbon.

3. Click Object in the Text group. Word displays the Object dialog box.

4. Click on the Create from File tab.

Use the controls on the dialog box to locate a sound file that you want included with your document. Choose "**Display Icon**"

Click on OK. An icon that looks like a speaker is inserted in your document.

You can later listen to the sound file(s) by simply double-clicking on the speaker icon.

Just keep in mind that at some point before the last version, I would remove all the sound files in all versions before it leaves the firm by email etc. You don't want "internal dialog" being listened to by outside sources. Nevertheless, the ability to do this gives the attorney an additional tool and can save them time.

........*

Working With Small Caps

Certain documents make use of small caps in the following ways: 1) in the letterhead, 2) as a stylistic look of a way to start off each new paragraph by applying small caps to the first word of each paragraph such as the word Whereas, 3) as a look that is used when companies are mentioned throughout the document and in the signatures and on and on.

WHEREAS

When you have the use of Small Caps throughout a document it is a good idea to assign a character style whose sole function is to Small Cap any text that needs to have Small Caps applied.

1.	One thing that occurs often enough is the need to change case when using Small Caps on areas of text that are in Upper Case when Small Caps is applied.

2.	When Small Caps is applied to text that is initially in UPPERCASE, **there is no apparent change in the text** and therefore many an operator will take this as the attempt to apply Small Caps was **not successful**.

3.	It does not make a difference whether it was applied by use of a Character Style or manually highlighting the text when applying Small Caps.

4.	In order for the Small Caps to properly take effect, the text that is currently in ALL CAPS needs to be switched over to Initial Caps. The text which had Small Caps applied will then immediately take effect and will now reflect the attribute. And of course, in order to do this, just use Change Case.

5.	**Change Case**. In 2007-13 under the "Home Tab" you will see the "**Aa**" button towards the left side of the screen.

6.	You can cycle through the different aspects of the change case selection by using **Shift F3** as well as the **Change Case** button.

........*

Not Your Typical Watermark

This does happen. You need to know this. It has happened twice in a short period of time.

Scenario:

Attorney comes to the center. He has an Adobe PDF document. The attorney says please remove the Watermark.

You go to Watermark within Adobe Professional but it does not show any file being uploaded to cause the mark. There is also no Text being used within the watermark text "key in" area. So what is going on?

1.	The watermark was originally loaded in MS Word.

2.	When the PDF was electronically created from the Desktop, the watermark became part of the newly created PDF file. The PDF file of this kind is produced in layers. We can select the watermark layer and delete it on any page we need to.

3.   Go to the first page within the Adobe file that has a watermark you need to delete. Click on an area where you are clicking on the picture of the Watermark. You will see the border of the watermark activate.

4.   Go To **Tools, Advanced Editing Functions** and choose -**Touch-Up Object Tool**. If the Watermark border is active, then just press delete. If it is not, click on any area of the mark and when you see its border activate press delete.

5.   If you accidentally delete the text press Control Z for Undo and try again.

6.   If you cannot seem to click on the mark to activate its border, click on the regular text and tug it to the Left just a bit to expose the watermark. Click on the watermark and press delete. Make sure you shift the text back to the original position.

7.   Once you go to **Tools, Advanced Editing Functions** and choose -**Touch-Up Object Tool** you can go to the next watermark to be selected and delete without having to turn on the feature again and again.

........*

This is Another One of Those Temporary Dilemmas You Should Know About

Scenario: The operator is doing a cover page for a litigation document. The cover page will consist of a Caption Box created from a 3 column 4 row table as well as the Title of the document under the actual caption box such as Motion For Summary Judgment. Also, the cover page is using Vertical Alignment Center.

Upon looking at the Caption Box on the cover page in Print Layout view, all of the cells appear to be split apart height wise. Even the width of the columns seems to have greatly expanded.

1.   We look at the caption box that we copied within the actual document to place on the cover page. It looks **absolutely fine** in both **Draft** as well as **Print Layout View**.

2.   We go back to the cover page and not knowing why the table has split apart for lack of a better term, select the table and start looking under Paragraph for extra Before/After spacing as well as checking the Line Spacing to make sure that there is no Exact Line Spacing or Multi Line spacing that could have caused this problem. Upon looking, there is no before or after spacing and the Line Spacing is single as it should be.

3.   According to the print preview, it shows the split apart look and that is what I am going to get if I print it out.

4.   I go back to Page Layout and again look at the Vertical Alignment setting which should be Center for the cover page. It turns out that instead of being Vertical Alignment Center, it was set for Vertical Alignment Justified.

5.   Because the table had been pulled apart by that justified setting, it did not occur to us right off the bat that it was a vertical alignment issue since the table took up so

much of the page. It may have taken 30 minutes to solve, but it won't happen again. One more thing to file away.

........*

Line Numbering Stemming from the Header

This is one of those requests that crop up once in a while but if it is you who needs to deal with it, you will surely want to know how.

The situation: Line numbering places a number next to each line whether we are using single or double space. When we use line numbering, anytime that it comes across a table, there will be a gap in the line numbering until it gets past the table. Upon coming across plain text, it will again start to number picking up where it left off. Here is the problem: Some attorneys do not like the gaps as it pertains to not numbering tables. They want uniformity.

They want every page to be uniform so that for example every page has the numbers 1-25 page after page and all pages look the same uninterrupted no matter what is going on that page. So, in order to get around this problem that exists when using traditional line numbering, we will insert our own line numbering that will be consistent on every page no matter whether there is text or tables.

So, how do we go about setting this up?

1.	Open up your Header on Page 1 of the main part of the document.

2.	Create a Text Box while the Header is open.

3.	Double Click on the text box and size it approximately 8.50 inches long and 0.40 wide.

4.	Position the empty text box to the edge of the first instance of text on page 1 where the No. 1 in your text box will be. You can use the Control Key and the Directional Arrows for micro moving of the text box if need be. **Note:** once your Header is open you can position the text box with the numbers anywhere you need to. It will always be associated with the Header regardless of where you position the text box. You may need to copy the completed text box to the next header in the same section if using the Different First Page Option.

5.	I am going to assume that we are using double spacing for the paragraphs of the document. Go into the text box and type 1-25 and/or 1-27 with a hard return after each number. I say 1-25 or 27 because you may have variations with your top and bottom margins. Let us also assume that we are using 1 inch top and bottom.

After you type in the numbers highlight the contents of the text box by clicking inside the text box and doing Control A. Format the text box to have 12 Pts. after each number. Yes the text box should be using single space but 12 Pts. After. Also, choose Right Alignment for the numbers in the text box.

6. In my opinion, this method works best for Double Spaced documents. The line numbering should go up until it is right before the Footer area.

7. Last step is to remove the Lines of the Text Box. Double click on the border of the box and in the Format Text Box Dialog Box go to lines and select "**No Line**"

8. Make sure that your text box that stems from the Header repeats on each and every page so that the numbering acts as a template and every page has uninterrupted line numbering throughout the entire main portion of the document.

9. **Three things**: if you have a cover page, TOC, TOA, Index of Terms then you do not have to start the line numbering until the first page of the actual document. Some people might say, why don't you just use pre-lined paper? You can but pre-lined paper usually has a double red line after the numbers, you may not have numbered paper available and you may not have enough time to make a template type page to make your own pre-numbered paper.

Finally if you wish to make the page more aesthetically pleasing, you can do a page border that only uses the left and right (no top or bottom) where you place a double line on the left where the numbers will line up and a single line on the right for a more traditional look.

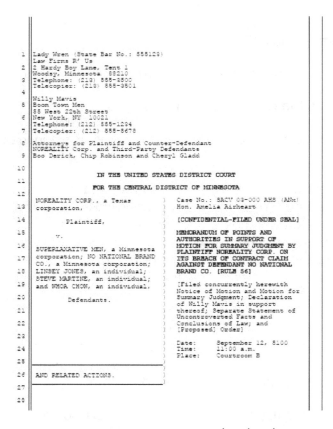

........*

From Portrait to Landscape to Portrait

I have seen many a situation where a Landscape Financial Table or Chart was placed in a document in landscape and then x number of copies needed to be made only to find that the page numbering that was continued from the portrait section is now still in the same position on the Landscape page that it was on the Portrait page thus being "way off center" on the Landscape page.

If it is a draft that needed to be distributed then not such a big deal but if not, someone is certainly going to spot that and it will have to be corrected and all copies would need to be reprinted.

So with that being said:

1.   You start off with Portrait and at some point there is for our example a very large financial table that needs to be inserted within the document. Now, you create a section break and then select Landscape for the Page Layout.

2.   Many people rely on the center tab that is part of the footer for the positioning of the page numbering. This is the reason why the numbering does not "**auto adjust**" when switching from portrait to Landscape. The center tab that appears on the ruler has to be tugged to the right in the ruler for the Landscape page number to appear centered.

3.   I usually like to just use the center button (icon) and not the center tab provided in the ruler of the footer. I just find it easier to deal with in terms of centering the page numbering in the footer. When you use the "**Center**" icon or (**Control E**), you guaranty that whether you are in portrait or landscape that your page numbering will automatically readjust to the center.

4.   Important to note that in some situations, the attorney will instruct you "not" to make a Landscape page but to instead stack the headings so what would you do with that large table if the table has 12 columns? We can do the following:

A.   You would take the first 6 headings and the numbers underneath and extract that piece from the table.

B.   Then, take the next 6 headings and the info underneath (the remaining Columns) and place that set underneath the first set of columns. In this way, the table exists within the Portrait format and that is referred to as stacking.

........*

My Table Of Contents Did Not Generate

This is the scenario: My TOC did not run. There are a multitude of different people who have had this same issue:

For those of you are using a third party software such as MacPac, Softwise, Payne etc. this may not be such an issue for you. For those generic users of MS Word, this is for you.

1.	First, the firms make use of the Heading Styles for the separate levels of a multi-level outline. Each Heading Style (Heading 1, 2, 3, etc.) is **Linked** to each separate level of the **Multi-Level Outline** through the "Link Level To Style" process that we do in the Multi-Level Dialog Box. You see the "Link Level To Style" option once you click on the "**More**" **Button** in the Multi-Level Dialog Box.

2.	When someone says my Table of Contents did not run, it could be for one of the following reasons:

A.	The levels and the Headings were not linked in the Multi-Level Dialog Box.

B.	The operator did not use the Heading Styles for each level but created their own. Although it will work, you would have to make sure you link each level to each style you created for each separate level.

C.	When you are about to run the Table of Contents, you should within the Table of Contents Dialog Box, go to "Options" and make sure that there is a level number next to those styles that are representing the different levels of the TOC you are about to run.

D.	Most TOC's are two levels. Therefore, under Options, within the TOC Dialog Box, there should be a "**1**" next to the style name representing the first level and a "**2**" next to the style representing the second level of your TOC. Those numbers determine how far in from the left margin each level will be positioned.

Next time your TOC does not run, go back to the basics and the reason will become apparent for the TOC failing to run properly.

We concentrate heavily on TOC, TOA, Index of Terms and Cross References in our classes so problems such as described in this article are common to us. This knowledge is essential in day to day word processing and essential in order to pass an MS Word Hands-On Agency or Law Firm Test.

........*

Things Not Apparent in MS Word:

Insert File is one of them:

People tend to not take notice about certain features until they are up against a time constraint of one type or another.

A while ago, I wrote about an operator who could not find "Insert File" and it caused a problem. It was hidden under **Insert** and **Object**. I certainly would have been fooled on that one as well. But the nature of 2007-13 is that there are features that are just not where you thought they would be.

If you are not solid using the new system then finding a feature like Change Case takes a while. In 2007-13 under the "Home Tab" you will see the "**Aa**" button towards the left side of the screen. Again, you may not realize what that button does right away, but nevertheless that is where it is. Those of you that could not find that button could resort to **Shift F3** to cycle through the Change Case Selections until you hit the one you want.

One thing that occurs often enough is the need to use change case when using the Small Caps attribute on areas of text that are in Upper Case when Small Caps is applied. When Small Caps is applied to a portion of text that is already in UPPERCASE, there is no apparent change in the text and therefore many an operator will take this as the attempt to apply Small Caps was not successful.

In order for the Small Caps to properly take effect, the text that is currently in ALL CAPS needs to be switched over to Initial Caps. The text which had Small Caps applied, will then immediately take effect and will now reflect the SMALL CAPS ATTRIBUTE. And of course, in order to do this, just use Change Case.

One more of those things not apparent. **Scenario:** The operator is doing a cover page for a litigation document. The cover page will consist of a Caption Box created from a 3 column 4 row table as well as the Title of the document under the actual caption box such as Motion For Summary Judgment. Also, the cover page is using Vertical Alignment Center.

Upon looking at the Caption Box on the cover page in Print Layout view, all of the cells appear to be split apart height wise. Even the width of the columns seems to have greatly expanded

1.   We look at the caption box that we copied within the actual document to place on the cover page. It looks absolutely fine in both Draft as well as Print Layout View.

2.   We go back to the cover page and not knowing why the table has split apart for lack of a better term, select the table and start looking under Paragraph for extra Before/After spacing as well as checking the Line Spacing to make sure that there is no Exact Line Spacing or Multi Line spacing that could have caused this problem. Upon looking, there is no before or after spacing and the Line Spacing is single as it should be.

3.   According to the print preview, it shows the split apart look and that is what I am going to get if I print it out.

4.   I go back to Page Layout and again and under Page Setup look at the Vertical Alignment setting which should be Center for the cover page. It turns out that instead of being Vertical Alignment Center, it was set for **Vertical Alignment Justified**.

5.   Because the table had been pulled apart by that Justified setting, it did not occur to us right off the bat that it was a vertical alignment issue since the table took up so much of the page. It may have taken 30 minutes to solve, but it won't happen again. One more thing to file away.

........*

Operator Gets Tripped By Legal Test and Their Own Habits

So , this is a true story that happened today but a good lesson was learned. Operator went for a Word Processing Test at a major law firm. The operator failed the test, but it should be said that this person is a very good operator but two things happened that caused her to unravel.

It involved the Multi-Level Outline. This firm did the following with the Levels for Headings 1-4.

Level 1 - Article I (Roman)

Level 2 - 1.

Level 3 - (a)

Level 4 - 1.01

Let's examine what caused the problems:

1.   The first thing that totally threw her that they placed the 1.01 (combo number) in Level 4. This is a typical law firm trainer trick where the trainer or WP person who wrote the test wants to **"trick you"** the test taker. To me, it makes no difference where the combo number comes in, but let us agree that having a 1.01 in Level 4 is not something you would likely see in a regular document. This unorthodox placement was 1 thing that caused confusion.

2.   The Roman in the First Level would initially come in as I.01 (Roman .01) until Legal Style is selected (in the Multi-Level Dialog Box) whereby the Roman number will now switch over to 1.01. The selection of Legal Style was never used.

3.   Finally, the operator had a secondary problem because nothing she was doing was taking effect. This was due to the fact that she did not initially Link Level 1 over to Heading 1, Link Level 2 to Heading 2, Link Level 3 to Heading 3 and Link Level 4 to Heading 4 (**in the Multi-Level Dialog Box**). It was not until way into the test that did it register, that Link Level To Style was not taken care of.

4.   So, when taking a test, look over the levels throughout the document before you start, plan your strategy, Link Level to Style for ALL levels (or at least 1-4) and do not let any out of the ordinary occurrence throw you off your game. Go about your business like you are at work. Relax, after all it is just word processing.

Control Shift S - Apply Styles Toolbar - A Third Source of Info Re Styles

I wanted to write about this because many times people overlook this valuable tool. For those of you working in WP centers or law firms for that matter, you will understand the significance of this great tool.

When I am either formatting a document from scratch or I am working on a large involved document, I like to work in Draft View so I can see the Style Tracking on the left side paragraph by paragraph. In Draft View, if you don't see your Left Side Tracking, go to File–Options–Advanced–Display and set Style Area for **1 inch**.

I also like to have my right side panel on as well so that I can have all of my styles visually available. It is all about information at your fingertips when you are styling a document.

The **Control Shift S** (Apply Styles Toolbar) comes into play for me when I want to instantly know what style the cursor is currently on. For example: I have worked on documents where there were a number of character styles being used within the document.

When I come across a Bolded Defined Term ("**Defined Term**"), right off the bat, I do not know whether it was bolded using **Direct Formatting** or whether it was bolded using a **Character Style**. If it was bolded by Direct Formatting, then when I place my cursor on the Defined Term the style name in the Apply Style Toolbar **will continue to display the paragraph style** associated with that paragraph. But, if the Defined Term was bolded with a Character Style, then as soon as I place my cursor on the Bolded area it will change over to the **Character Style name** in the Apply Style Toolbar. Give it a try yourself.

Other Great Reasons to use the Apply Style Toolbar:

1.	My left side tracking (under Draft View) only records (tracks) Paragraph type styles.

2.	The right side panel will highlight the current style you have your cursor on, but, you may have to look up and down along the style pallet until you see which style is highlighted.

3.	When the Apply Styles Toolbar is active, the second you place your cursor on a particular **paragraph** or **characters** that have a **Character Style** applied to them, the style name **will instantly show** in the small window of the **Apply Styles Toolbar**.

4.   With the **Apply Style Toolbar**, you also have the ability to immediately modify the style, create a new style, (paragraph or character) or type in the top window until a desired style is found and then simply press your return button to apply that style.

Next time you are editing a large file, bring the Apply Styles Toolbar up for a third source of info.

When working in a legal environment, the more info you have at your fingertips the better!

RUNNING A TABLE OF CONTENTS IN TWO COLUMNS - Bonus - Bonus - Bonus

This subject will come up from time to time at work and it will come up from time to time on a hands on word processing test. Running your TOC in a two column format is rather simple but it does have a routine that needs to be followed so let's go over it. Of course, we are using the "Heading" styles to represent each separate Multilevel Outline Level of our document.

Most of the time, this is being done because the document is rather large and instead of having 5 pages of Table of Contents entries they want to significantly shorten it. Because of this, we would be wise to use the Table of Contents method where the **TOC has it own dedicated section** and the Table of Contents and Page Heading is placed in the **Header** of that Section.

So let's get this going.

1.   In your document, after your cover page, we have a section break. Now your TOC comes in. After your TOC make a section break. Your Table of Contents Heading will be placed in the **First Page Header of Section 2**. When it spills over one page the **Second Header of Section 2** (because of the different first page option) will be set-up to say **Table of Contents (continued)** as shown in the pictures below.

TABLE·OF·CONTENTS¶

Page¶

First Page Header -Section 2-

TABLE·OF·CONTENTS¶
(continued)¶

Page¶

Header -Section 2-

Section Break (Next Page)

2.   Now that your heading is in place, we can focus on the running of the Table of Contents. **Run the Table of Contents as usual**. The picture at the top of the next page assumes you just ran your Table of Contents.

3.   Two things to do in **TOC 1, TOC 2 and TOC 3**. My sample happens to have 3 sections that are utilized in the TOC but **most** will have two. You can enter TOC 1 TOC 2 and TOC 3, by **double clicking** on the style name in the left side panel as long as you are in **Draft** view

4.   In **each** of the above-mentioned TOC sections, I want you to modify them and change the **font** down to **8pt**. Then go **Tabs**, and under **Tabs** **clear out** the current Tab that controls the page numbers and replace it with a **Tab at 3.0** on the ruler. Make sure the Tab is set for "**Right Tab**" and apply a **dotted line leader** which is number **2**. as shown in the picture below.

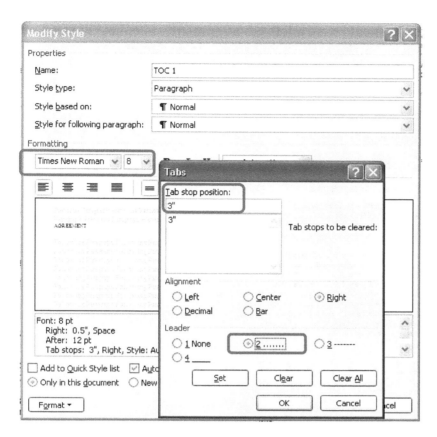

5.　　　Keep in mind that **after each heading**, there is a tab before the **words of that heading** so that has to be adjusted as well. So let me show you how that would look. In our example, if you look back a page, the two tab situation, did not come into play **until TOC 2** but many times there will be a heading number followed by text on **TOC 1** as well.

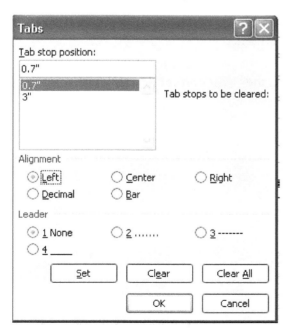

6.   The **0.7** example, should have **a left tab alignment** while the **3.0** which represents and controls **the page numbers on the right**, should **have right alignment and a dotted line leader attached to it.**

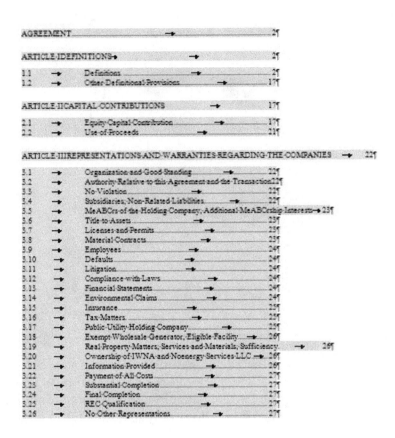

7.   Okay, we have **not** put on the Columns feature yet. Above, your TOC should look something like this sample at this point. Do not worry too much about those areas that jut out because when we create the two column look, they will correct themselves.

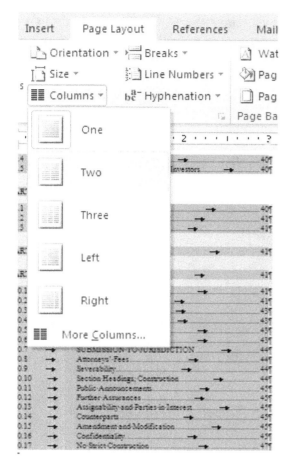

8.   As shown above, **highlight the entire TOC** then go to Page Layout, Columns and select Two.

9.   When you select Two, your TOC will divide into two columns and you will still have the word "Page" in your header but it will only **be on one side** and **not** the left side as shown below.

TABLE·OF·CONTENTS·¶

11.	There are **two ways to go** as to the word **"Page"**. We can either 1) delete the word Page altogether or we can create **a two column one row table** in the **header** and place the word **"Page"** over each set of page numbers in the TOC. Let us assume that we have decided to place the word **"Page"** over **both sets of numbers** for the TOC pages.

12.	In your header, make a **two column 1 row table**. In each cell of the table, do **Control R** and type in **"Page"**. That will throw the word **"Page"** to the **extreme right** of each cell. Now, manipulate the cells so that the word Page from each cell sits nicely over the page numbers. Take a look at the picture below, and note that I took off the borders of the table that contains the word Page in each cell.

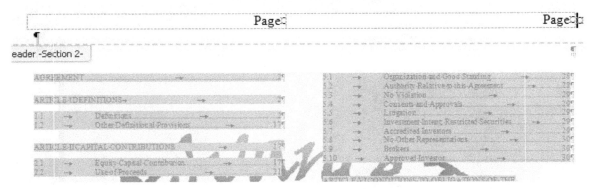

13.	Finally, when dealing with columns, you should know that when you are in **Draft view**, the columns will appear as **one long column**. If for any reason, you need to break the column up **at a different location** than it is currently breaking, then while in Draft view, you do **Control Shift Enter** and that is a **column break** which is what you use to segment a column as needed. Most probably you will not have to use this.

Conclusion:

Well, I see you made it. If you have purchased Volumes 1 and 2 you have now absorbed and have been exposed to close to 100 articles, scenarios and solutions. Just being exposed to all those different solutions will cause you to have questions and comments. If you have questions pertaining to all of the subject matter that was covered thus far, you are welcome to email me at **louisellman@gmail.com**, **louis@advanceto.com** and/or go to **www.legaltestready.com** and go to the Press Conference Page and ask your questions. I will be happy to assist you.

If you should need basic through advanced legal word processing training or just plain MS Word training we have thorough courses that we give both in person and by phone. We also go to offices and teach staff. I take part regularly in developing testing and training materials for job agencies, law firms and other corporations. Feel free to contact us about these services as well.

The combination of these books and our training produce operators and secretaries that are much more aware of the system as a whole. They also develop true strategic skills and are very good at looking at a particular document and sizing it up quickly as to formatting, outlines, styles, sections etc.

There will be a Volume 3 of this series soon and we move on in further educating and ever increasing our awareness level.

Thank you again for purchasing these books and I hope you have benefitted from them.

Best Regards,

Louis